LINES ON THE UNDERGROUND

an anthology
for Bakerloo & Jubilee Line travellers

Compiled by

DOROTHY MEADE & TATIANA WOLFF

*Illustrated by Basil Cottle
and Jonathan Newdick*

CASSELL

Cassell Publishers Limited
Wellington House, 125 Strand
London WC2R 0BB

in association with the London Transport Museum

This edition published 1996
The material in this anthology was first published in
Lines on the Underground, 1994

British Library Cataloguing in Publication Data
A catalogue record for this book is available from the British Library

ISBN 0-304-34861-9

Distributed in Australia by
Capricorn Link (Australia) Pty Ltd
2/13 Carrington Road, Castle Hill, NSW 2154

Printed and bound in Great Britain by Hillman Printers Ltd

To Joe, Dora, Anna and Ben

*

And in memory of
M. M. W.

BAKERLOO LINE

Elephant & Castle

Change for Northern line

In the south suburbs at the Elephant
Is best to lodge.

WILLIAM SHAKESPEARE, *Twelfth Night*, 1601

The Elephant and Castle Underground Station (Northern and Bakerloo Lines) is haunted by the sound of running footsteps. These are frequently heard by maintenance staff working there after services have stopped, especially on wintry nights. When the Victoria Line was being built it was necessary to make a new tunnel beneath the Thames close to Vauxhall Bridge. The navvies who excavated this in 1968 firmly believed in the ghost many of them met in the dark gloom. Irishmen working on the project called him 'The Quare Feller' and one described him as being at least seven feet tall, with outstretched, menacing, hands and arms. They believed that they had disturbed one of the Plague pits of 1665.

J.A. BROOKS, *Ghosts of London*, 1982

Lambeth North

This was the London of my childhood, of my moods and awakenings: memories of Lambeth in the spring; of trivial incidents and things; of riding with Mother on top of a horse-bus trying to touch passing lilac-trees – of the many coloured bus tickets, orange, blue, pink and green, that bestrewed the pavement where the trams and buses stopped – of rubicund flower-girls at the corner of Westminster Bridge, making gay *boutonnières*, their adroit fingers manipulating tinsel and quivering fern – of the humid odour of freshly watered roses that affected me with a vague sadness – of melancholy Sundays and pale-faced parents and their children escorting toy windmills and coloured balloons over Westminster Bridge; and the maternal penny steamers that softly lowered their funnels as they glided under it. From such trivia I believe my soul was born.

CHARLIE CHAPLIN, *My Autobiography*, 1964

Waterloo
Change for Northern line

Every man has his Moscow. Suppose he [John Brown] did fail, every man meets his Waterloo at last.

WENDELL PHILLIPS, Speech on Harper's Ferry, 1 November 1859

. . . on Waterloo Bridge . . . The wind has blown up the waves. The river races beneath us, and the men standing on the barges have to lean all their weight on the tiller. A black tarpaulin is tied down over a swelling load of gold. Avalanches of coal glitter blackly. As usual, painters are slung on planks across the great riverside hotels, and the hotel windows have already points of light in them. On the other side the city is white as if with age; St. Paul's swells white above the fretted, pointed, or oblong buildings beside it. The cross alone shines rosy-gilt.

VIRGINIA WOOLF, *Jacob's Room*, 1922

Embankment
Change for Circle, District and Northern lines

Here was the city, the world. I waited for the flowering to come to me. The trams on the Embankment sparked blue. The river was edged and pierced with reflections of light, blue and red and yellow. Excitement!

V.S. NAIPAUL, *The Mimic Men*, 1967

. . . they set off resolutely along the desolate Embankment homeward.
But indeed the Thames was a wonderful sight that year! Ice-fringed along either shore, and with drift-ice in the middle reflecting a luminous scarlet from the broad red setting sun, and moving steadily, inces-

santly seaward. A swarm of mewing gulls went to and fro, and with them mingled pigeons and crows. The buildings on the Surrey side were dim and grey and very mysterious, the moored, ice-blocked barges silent and deserted, and here and there a lit window shone warm. The sun sank right out of sight into a bank of blue, and the Surrey side dissolved in mist save for a few insoluble spots of yellow light, that presently became many. And after our lovers had come under Charing Cross Bridge the Houses of Parliament rose before them at the end of a great crescent of golden lamps, blue and faint, halfway between the earth and sky. And the clock on the Tower was like a November sun.

H.G. WELLS, *Love and Mr Lewisham*, 1900

Charing Cross
Change for Jubilee and Northern lines

That the First Charles does here in triumph ride,
See his son reign'd where he a martyr died . . .

EDMUND WALLER, 'On the Statue of King Charles I at
Charing Cross, in the year 1674'

. . . Comely and calm, he rides
Hard by his own Whitehall:
Only the night wind glides:
No crowds, nor rebels, brawl.

LIONEL JOHNSON, 'By the statue of King Charles I at
Charing Cross', *Poems*, 1895

. . . upon thy so sore loss
Shall shine the traffic of Jacob's ladder
Pitched betwixt Heaven and Charing Cross . . .

FRANCIS THOMPSON, 'The Kingdom of God',
The Works, 1913

Out of the dark sky a noise was coming, a droning sound. The streets were empty, there was no light. Leaves blown across the pavement brushed our ankles and moved on, fleeing along the wind.

'Charing Cross Underground. Let's go there,' I said, urgently. Grasping our blankets we stumbled across the forecourt of Charing Cross

Station, and down the side street. Suddenly our path was brilliantly lit, bathed in icy white light. . . .

'What's happening?' she cried to me.

'Those enemy flares, parachute flares, shot out by our gunners. They are trying to get light to bomb by. Come on, come quickly now!' . . . It was full there, crowded with people even on the District Line platforms and approaches, which weren't really deep enough to be safe.

JILL PATON WALSH, *The Fireweed*, 1969

Piccadilly Circus
Change for Piccadilly line

If the present ballooning mania should be carried much further, it will become necessary for the Police Commissioners to issue regulations as to the taking up and setting down, in the same way as they now do with regard to carriages. . . . It is difficult to go down Piccadilly after six o'clock p.m., without getting your eyes filled with sand thrown out by the occupants of a balloon car, who, making themselves as jolly as sand-boys, sprinkle London with their discharged ballast.

Punch, 1849

Then a sentimental passion of a vegetable fashion must excite your
languid spleen,
An attachment *à la* Plato for a bashful young potato, or a not too
French French bean!
Though the Philistines may jostle, you will rank as an apostle in the
high aesthetic band,
If you walk down Piccadilly with a poppy or a lily in your mediaeval
hand.

W.S. GILBERT, *Patience*, 1881

Piccadilly! Shops, palaces, bustle, and breeze,
The whirring of wheels, and the murmur of trees;
By night or by day, whether noisy or stilly,
Whatever my mood is, I love Piccadilly.

F. LOCKER-LAMPSON, *London Lyrics*, 1857

Oxford Circus
Change for Central and Victoria lines

So then, Oxford-street, stonyhearted stepmother! thou that listenest to the sighs of orphans, and drinkest the tears of children, at length I was dismissed from thee: . . .

. . . oftentimes on moonlight nights, during my first mournful abode in London, my consolation was (if such it could be thought) to gaze from Oxford-street up every avenue in succession which pierces through the heart of Marylebone to the fields and the woods.

THOMAS DE QUINCEY, *Confessions of an English Opium-Eater*, 1822

Regent's Park

'Verily I cannot get this mighty street out of my head,' said the Doctor. 'And then there is the new park – what do you call it? Mary-le-bone – no, the Regent's Park: it seems to be an elegant, well-planned place, methinks, and will have a fine effect, no doubt, with its villas and what not, when the shrubs and trees have shot up a little. But I shall not live to see it, and I care not; for I remember those fields in their natural, rural garb, covered with herds of kine, when you might stretch across from old William's farm there a-top of Portland Street, right away without impediment to Saint John's Wood, where I have gathered blackberries when a boy – which pretty place, I am sorry to see, these brick and mortar gentry have trenched upon. Why, Ephraim, your metropolitans will have half a day's journey, if you proceed at this rate, ere you can get a mouthful of fresh air.'

EPHRAIM HARDCASTLE, *Wine and Walnuts;
or, After Dinner Chit-Chat*, 1823

They were by this time outside the lovely gate; they went legging it down the short serpentine road that, with trees, railings and air of a private avenue, runs downhill from the Inner into the Outer Circle. Ahead one had still an illusion of wooded distance, out of whose blue and bronzy ethereality rose the tops of Regency terraces – these, in their semi-ruin, just less pale than the sky. . . . This moment of walking to meet the houses seemed to have its place in no given hour of time – though across it, in contradiction, St. Marylebone clock began striking eight.

ELIZABETH BOWEN, *The Heat of the Day*, 1949

Baker Street

Change for Circle, Hammersmith & City, Jubilee and Metropolitan lines

For those of us who did not live in it, the London of the eighties and nineties of last century is simply the London of Holmes and we cannot pass down Baker Street without thinking of him and trying to locate his lodgings. Of whom but Holmes has a literature sprung up solely concerned with the question of where he lived?

HESKETH PEARSON, *Conan Doyle: His Life and Art*, 1943

Marylebone

. . . we abroad to Marrowbone and there walked in the garden, the first time I ever there, and a pretty place it is; and here we eat and drank and stayed till 9 at night; and so home by moonshine . . .

SAMUEL PEPYS, *Diary, 7 May 1668*

PEACHUM: The Captain keeps too good company ever to grow rich. Marybone* and the chocolate-houses are his undoing . . .

MACHEATH: There will be deep play to-night at Marybone, and consequently money may be picked up upon the road. Meet me there, and I'll give you the hint who is worth setting.

* The Marylebone Pleasure Gardens.

JOHN GAY, *The Beggar's Opera*, 1728

Advertisement of Marylebone gardens: 'Mr. Trusler's daughter begs leave to inform the Nobility and Gentry, that she intends to make fruit-tarts during the fruit season; and hopes to give equal satisfaction as with the rich cakes, and almond cheesecakes. The fruit will always be fresh gathered, having great quantities in the garden; and none but loaf sugar used, and the finest Epping butter.'

The Daily Advertiser, 6 May 1760, quoted in
J.T. SMITH, *A Book for a Rainy Day*, 1845

That afternoon Hetta trusted herself all alone to the mysteries of the Marylebone underground railway,* and emerged with accuracy at King's Cross . . .

* The Metropolitan underground railway, which had opened in 1863.

ANTHONY TROLLOPE, *The Way We Live Now*, 1875

Between 1871 and 1872, openings were made in the crown of the long tunnel, venting through iron grilles at the centre of Euston and Marylebone Roads. . . . The author's father . . . used to recall that these grilles afforded a lunchtime diversion for the younger clerks, whose custom was to keep them under close surveillance. The reason for this was that should any lady be unwise enough to stand over them whilst a train was passing below, the force of the blast would raise her skirts in a satisfyingly revealing fashion.

ALAN A. JACKSON, *London's Metropolitan Railway*, 1986

Edgware Road

. . . 'tis certain, that this was formerly the only or the main Road from London to *St Alban's*, being the famous high Road call'd *Watling-street*, which reached from *London* to *Shrewsbury*, and on towards Wales.*

*In a later edition this sentence was added: 'The remains of this road are still to be seen here, and particularly in this, that from Hide-Park Corner, just where Tyburn stands, the road makes one straight line without any turning, even to the very town of St Albans.'

DANIEL DEFOE, *A Tour thro' the Whole Island of Great Britain*, 1742

I'm sure if anyone had told me as I could be whisked away from Moorfields to Marrybone in ten minutes I should have said, 'Go along with your rubbish' . . . just as a train as was a-goin' to start, and afore as I'd time to wink, as the sayin' is, I was shoved head foremost into a carriage and away we went under them dark arches . . .

. . . I set a-waitin' till a party put his head in at the winder and said, 'Change here for Kensington.'

I says, 'I shan't do nothin' of the sort, for I'm a-goin' to Baker-street.' 'Then,' says he, 'you've come past it; you must go upstairs and get a ticket to go back.'

I says, 'What a shame to bring parties out of their way like this.' He says, 'Can't you read nor got no ears, for,' he says, 'the names of the stations is wrote up.' . . .

I must say as we was not long in bein' whisked to Baker Street, where the train put us out, tho' in that 'urried way, as it's a mercy I didn't fall out thro' a-ketchin' my foot in a party's crinoline as was next the door.

ARTHUR SKETCHLEY, 'Mrs Brown on the Underground Railway', *The Brown Papers*, second series, reprinted from 'Fun', 1870

Paddington
Change for Circle, District and Hammersmith & City lines

I am a broken-hearted milkman, in grief I'm arrayed,
Through keeping of the company of a young servant maid,
Who lived on board wages to keep the house clean
In a gentleman's family near Paddington Green.

Chorus:
>   She was as beautiful as a butterfly
>   And as proud as a Queen
>   Was pretty Polly Perkins of
>   Paddington Green.

Her eyes were as black as the pips of a pear,
No rose in the garden with her cheeks could compare,
Her hair hung in ringlets so beautiful and long,
I thought that she loved me but I found I was wrong.
. . .
In six months she married, this hard-hearted girl,
But it was not a wicount, and it was not a nearl,
It was not a baronite, but a shade or two wuss,
It was a bow-legged conductor of a Twopenny Bus.

Victorian Street Ballads edited by W. Henderson, 1937

Warwick Avenue

Little Venice [served by Warwick Avenue station]. The canal surrounded by trees . . . [is] one of the most unexpected beauty spots in
London. Though both Robert Browning* and Lord Byron compared it
to Venice, the name seems not to have been generally used until after
the 2nd World War.

* Robert Browning lived at 19 Warwick Crescent between 1861 and 1887.

The London Encyclopaedia edited by Ben Weinreb
and Christopher Hibbert, 1983

Maida Vale

>   I know where Maida Vale receives
> The night dews on her summer leaves,
> Nor less my settled spirit cleaves
>   To Bloomsbury.

ANON., 'To Bloomsbury' quoted in *London in Verse*
edited by Christopher Logue, 1982

Kilburn Park

. . . 'Don't you ever get bored?' Toni once asked as we were adding up the months and years of our lives we had spent on trains. He only had a ten-stop ride round the Circle Line: uneventful, all underground, no chance of rape or abduction.

'Nah. Too much going on.'

'Tunnels, bridges, telegraph poles?'

'That sort of thing. No, actually, things like Kilburn. It's Doré; it really is.'

The next half-day, Toni came to try it out. Between Finchley Road and Wembley Park the train goes over a high viaduct system at Kilburn. . . . The value of Kilburn depended on not knowing particularities, because it changed to the eye and the brain according to yourself, your mood and the day. On a late afternoon in winter, with the egg-white lamps faintly beginning to show, it was melancholy and frightening, the haunt of acid-bath murderers. On a clear, bright morning in summer, with almost no smog and lots of people visible, it was like a brave little slum in the Blitz: you half expected to see George VI poking around the few remaining bomb-sites with his umbrella. . . .

Toni and I got off at Wembley Park, changed platforms, and went back over the area. Then we did the same again.

JULIAN BARNES, *Metroland*, 1980

Queen's Park

. . . so low were the finances [of Queen's Park Rangers] in these early days that the club's gear consisted of four uprights and two pieces of tape used as cross-bars! The question of shorts was also acute, but one supporter who maintained riding stables at Maida Vale came to the rescue by giving all the players a pair of riding pants in which they played their first match! . . .

The Kensal Rise ground was requisitioned for allotments, but salvation came when in 1917 Shepherd's Bush amateur club disbanded and Rangers took over their ground at Loftus Road. They were 'home' at last. . . .

R.J. HAYTER, *Official History of Queen's Park Rangers*, 1948

Kensal Green

My friends, we will not go again or ape an ancient rage,
Or stretch the folly of your youth to be the shame of age,
But walk with clearer eyes and ears this path that wandereth,
And see undrugged in evening light the decent inn of death;
For there is good news yet to hear and fine things to be seen,
Before we go to Paradise by way of Kensal Green.

G.K. CHESTERTON, 'The Rolling English Road', 1914

Willesden Junction

Willesden Junction Station. . . . There is here almost as great a network of railways as at Clapham Junction, the lines radiating hence to almost all parts of London both north and south of the Thames; and the arrangement of the station is, if possible, more consummately bewildering to the unhappy traveller who has to 'change'.

E. WALFORD, *Greater London*, 1882–4

. . . the pilgrimage to *Our Lady of Willesden*, a popular pilgrimage resembling the more famous one to Our Lady of Walsingham . . . and to it the Londoners of both sexes flocked in great numbers, it being in the 15th century their most favourite resort. But the pilgrims were, at least in the later years, often persons of immoral character; and the pilgrimage itself was the occasion of much scandal. 'Ye men of London,' said the Scottish friar Father Donald, in a sermon he preached at St Paul's Cross . . . 'gang you yourselves with your wives to Willesden, in the Devyl's name, or else keep them at home with you with sorrow.' The pilgrimage was suppressed and the miraculous image of Our Lady of Willesden was destroyed at Chelsea, along with the shrine of Our Lady of Walsingham, in 1548.

JAMES THORNE, *Handbook to the Environs of London*, 1876

Harlesden

Harlesden was recorded as *Herulvestune* in Domesday Book and comes from the personal name of the Saxon *Heoruwulf* . . . and Old English tun, 'a farm' – . . . being on a site where he and his family once lived. It was recorded as *Herlesdon* in 1291.

CYRIL M. HARRIS, *What's in a Name?*, 1977

Stonebridge Park

It was here that the Harrow Road was carried across the River Brent and the local inn – the Coach and Horses – was frequented by the painter, Morland, at the end of the 18th century. . . . The development of the Stonebridge Park estate in the 1870s and 1880s was intended to set the tone of the area. . . .

The London Encyclopaedia edited by Ben Weinreb
and Christopher Hibbert, 1983

Wembley Central

When melancholy Autumn comes to Wembley
And electric trains are lighted after tea
The poplars near the Stadium are trembly
With their tap and tap and whispering to me,
Like the sound of little breakers
Spreading out along the surf-line
When the estuary's filling
With the sea.

JOHN BETJEMAN, 'Harrow-on-the-Hill',
A Few Late Chrysanthemums, 1954

Oh bygone Wembley! Where's the pleasure now?
The temples stare, the Empire passes by.
This was the grandest Palace of them all.

The British government pavilion and the famous Wembley lions.
Now they guard an empty warehouse site.

JOHN BETJEMAN, 'Metro-Land' (TV programme), 1973, quoted in
The Best of Betjeman selected by John Guest, 1978

North Wembley

Gentle Brent, I used to know you
  Wandering Wembley-wards at will,
Now what change your waters show you
  In the meadowlands you fill!
Recollect the elm-trees misty
And the footpath climbing twisty
Under cedar-shaded palings,
  Low laburnum-leaned-on railings,
  Out of Northolt on and upwards to the heights of Harrow hill.

JOHN BETJEMAN, 'Middlesex',
A Few Late Chrysanthemums, 1954

South Kenton

. . . on the northern part of Kenton lane in 1933 . . . the builder of the houses, a man named Jefferies, would go round on a Sunday, when people came to visit the site, and offer to lend them the £5 deposit money! 'Houses on gently moulded hills, surrounded by verdant lanes and age-old trees, giving quiet, pastoral beauty. This is the ideal setting for one's home.' Even today some of this sylvan beauty remains.

DENNIS EDWARDS AND RON PIGRAM,
London's Underground Suburbs, 1986

Kenton

Since I had the pleasure of seeing you last I have been almost wholly in the country at a farmer's house quite alone trying to write a Comedy [*She Stoops to Conquer*]. It is now finished but when or how it will be acted, or whether it will be acted at all are questions I cannot resolve.

OLIVER GOLDSMITH, letter to Bennet Langton, 4 September 1771,
quoted in *The Collected Letters of Oliver Goldsmith* edited by
Katharine C. Balderston, 1928

The farmhouse still stands on a gentle eminence in what is called Hyde-Lane, leading to Kenton . . . and looking over a pretty country in the direction of Hendon; and when a biographer of the poet went in search of it some years since . . . he found traditions of Goldsmith surviving too . . . how Reynolds and Johnson and Sir William Chambers had been entertained there, and he had taken the young folks of the farm in a coach to see some strolling players at Hendon; how he had come home one night without his shoes, having left them stuck fast in a slough; and how he had an evil habit of reading in bed, and of putting out his candle by flinging his slipper at it. It was certain he was fond of this humble place.

JOHN FORSTER, *The Life and Adventures of Oliver Goldsmith*, 1848

> There's a storm cloud to the westward over Kenton,
> There's a line of harbour lights at Perivale,
> Is it rounding rough Pentire in a flood of sunset fire
> The little fleet of trawlers under sail?
> Can those boats be only roof tops
> As they stream along the skyline
> In a race for port and Padstow
> With the gale?

JOHN BETJEMAN, 'Harrow-on-the-Hill',
A Few Late Chrysanthemums, 1954

Harrow & Wealdstone

> Then Harrow-on-the-Hill's a rocky island
> And Harrow churchyard full of sailors' graves
> And the constant click and kissing of the trolley buses hissing
> Is the level to the Wealdstone turned to waves
> And the rumble of the railway
> Is the thunder of the rollers
> As they gather up for plunging
> Into caves.

JOHN BETJEMAN, 'Harrow-on-the-Hill',
A Few Late Chrysanthemums, 1954

Anthony Trollope and his family once lived in a farmhouse in Harrow Weald. . . . Trollope has nothing good to say about Harrow, to which he tramped day after day, at first from the Weald, then from Orley Farm – 12 miles through the lanes. . . .

. . . Grimsdyke . . . containing a Norman Shaw mansion, formerly the home of W.S. Gilbert . . . Gilbert loved this place; he was passionately fond of birds and animals; game birds flourished here, and he would not allow his keepers to shoot even a squirrel . . . he enjoyed the seclusion of his fine library (into which bullfinches and even deer would penetrate), and the splendour of the music room, with its minstrels gallery. When the great house was sold, dozens of pictures of characters from the Savoy operas were found, and the headman's block and the axe from the *Yeoman of the Guard*.

BRUCE STEVENSON, *Middlesex*, 1972

JUBILEE LINE

Charing Cross
Change for Bakerloo and Northern lines

Undone, undone the lawyers are,
   They wander about the towne,
Nor can find the way to Westminster,
   Now Charing-cross is downe:
At the end of the Strand they make a stand,
   Swearing they are at a loss,
And chaffing say, that's not the way,
   They must go by Charing-cross.

'The Downfall of Charing-Cross', T. Percy's
Reliques of Ancient English Poetry, 1765

. . . the great railway station of which a bygone poet sang:
  'The terminus of Charing Cross
    Is haunted, when it rains,
  By Nymphs, who there a shelter seek,
    And wait for mythic trains.'

ARTHUR M. BINSTEAD, *Pitcher in Paradise* 1903

> . . . Trafalgar Square
> (The fountains volleying golden glaze)
> Gleams like an angel-market. High aloft
> Over his couchant Lions in a haze
> Shimmering and bland and soft,
> A dust of chrysoprase,
> Our Sailor takes the golden gaze
> Of the slanting sun, and flames superb
> As once he flamed it on his ocean round.

W.E. HENLEY, 'London Voluntaries',
London Voluntaries . . . and Other Verses, 1893

Green Park
Change for Piccadilly and Victoria lines

I have a weakness for the convenient, familiar, treeless, or almost treeless, expanse of the Green Park, and the friendly part it plays as a kind
of encouragement to Piccadilly. I am so fond of Piccadilly that I am
grateful to any one or anything that does it a service.

HENRY JAMES, 'London', *English Hours*, 1905

Bond Street
Change for Central line

> All Sublunary things of Death partake;
> What Alteration does a Cent'ry make?
> Kings and Comedians all are mortal found,
> *Caesar* and *Pinkethman* are under Ground.
> What's not destroy'd by Time's devouring Hand?
> Where's *Troy*, and where's the *May-pole* in the *Strand*?
> Pease, Cabbages, and Turnips once grew, where
> Now stand new *Bond-Street*, and a newer Square;
> Such Piles of Buildings now rise up and down,
> *London* itself seems going out of *Town*.

JAMES BRAMSTON, *The Art of Politicks, In Imitation of Horace's Art of Poetry*,
1729 (published anonymously)

Old Bond street where, 'at the silk bag shop' in 1768, Laurence Sterne breathed his last. He murmured: 'Now it is come,' and then 'put up his hand as if to stop a blow, and died in a minute'. His servants rifled his possessions and made off with everything they could carry. It is said that even his body was stolen. It was dug up by the Resurrection men, at dead of night, and sold to an anatomist. While it was in the process of being dissected, the anatomist was joined by a colleague. As luck would have it, he was one of Sterne's life-long friends. He glanced at the corpse and fainted.

PETER BUSHELL, *London's Secret History*, 1983

Bond Street fascinated her; Bond Street early in the morning in the season; its flags flying; its shops; no splash; no glitter; one roll of tweed in the shop where her father had bought his suits for fifty years; a few pearls; salmon on an iceblock.

VIRGINIA WOOLF, *Mrs Dalloway*, 1925

I like to walk down Bond street, thinking of all the things I don't desire.

LOGAN PEARSALL SMITH, *Afterthoughts*, 1931

At Bond Street a lot of people get out, and the train stays still long enough to read comfortably the poem provided by the Keepers of the Underground, inserted into a row of advertisements.

DORIS LESSING, 'In Defence of the Underground', *London Observed*, 1992

Baker Street
Change for Bakerloo, Circle, Hammersmith & City and Metropolitan lines

Ladies, are you aware that the great Pitt lived in Baker Street?

WILLIAM MAKEPEACE THACKERAY, *Vanity Fair*, 1847–8

St. John's Wood

> The fields from Islington to Marybone,
> To Primrose Hill and Saint John's Wood,
> Were builded over with pillars of gold,
> And there Jerusalem's pillars stood.

WILLIAM BLAKE, *Jerusalem: The Emanation of the Giant Albion*, 1804–20

. . . this was a district which no Forsyte entered without open disapproval and secret curiosity.

JOHN GALSWORTHY, *The Man of Property*, 1906

I had entered the precincts of St. John's Wood; and as I went past its villas of coquettish aspect, with gay Swiss gables, with frivolously Gothic or Italian or almost Oriental faces, their lighter outlook on existence, the air they have of not taking life too seriously, began to exert an influence.

St. John's Wood is the home in fiction of adventuresses and profligacy and outrageous supper-parties.

LOGAN PEARSALL SMITH, *More Trivia*, 1921

They had gone to live in St. John's Wood, that airy uphill neighbourhood where the white and buff-coloured houses, pilastered or gothic, seem to have been built in a grove. A fragrant, faint impropriety, orris-dust of a century, still hangs over part of this neighbourhood; glass passages lead in from high green gates, garden walls are mysterious, laburnums falling between the windows and walls have their own secrets. Acacias whisper at nights round airy, ornate little houses in which pretty women lived singly but were not always alone. In the unreal late moonlight you might hear a ghostly hansom click up the empty road, or see on a pale wall the shadow of an opera cloak.

ELIZABETH BOWEN, *To the North*, 1932

Swiss Cottage

Bulletin No. 1

GREETINGS to our nightly companions, our temporary cave dwellers, our sleeping companions, somnambulists, snorers, chatterers and all who inhabit the Swiss Cottage station of the Bakerloo nightly from dusk to dawn.

This is the first in a series of announcements, issued in the name of co-operation, so that we may find what comfort and amenities there may be in this our nightly place of refuge.

Bulletin No. 2

EXPERT ADVICE: Vibration due to heavy gunfire or other causes will be felt much less if you do not lie with your head against the wall.

Bulletin No. 3

WITHOUT COMMENT: Our sleeping companions last night were a boy of six and his sister of nine. When the All Clear was sounded at 6.30 they said, 'We are going home now to a nice breakfast.' 'Not to sleep?' 'Oh yes! We go to sleep then, until twelve or half-past. Then about two o'clock we come back and wait until they let us into the station at four o'clock.'

WARBLING NOTE OF VARYING PITCH: One thousand five hundred and three people slept in this station-shelter the other evening. 1,503! 1,650 of whom seemed to be snoring. And the Government is distributing *ear*-plugs!

THE SWISS COTTAGER, *De Profundis*, Organ of the Air Raid Shelterers at Swiss Cottage Station, London NW3, September 1940

Finchley Road

Change for Metropolitan line

I am a lucky Londoner, born in the Finchley Road, where Hampstead meets St. John's Wood; the old boundary stone still stood in our garden. For 20 years I lived in Kensington (naturally), and am now to be found in an area known to its residents as Bedford Park, Chiswick, Turnham Green or Acton, according to mood or political affiliation.

MICHAEL FLANDERS in Foreword to *London Between the Lines* compiled by John Bishop and Virginia Broadbent, 1973

West Hampstead

I am in the little roads [in West Hampstead] full of houses. . . . The streets here are classically inclined. Agamemnon, Achilles, Ulysses, and there is Orestes Mews . . . one may postulate an army man, classically educated, who was given the job of naming these streets. In fact, this was not so far wrong. The story was this. . . . An ex-army man, minor gentry, had a wife in the country with many children, and a mistress in town, with many more. To educate all these he went in for property, bought farmland that spread attractively over a hill with views of London, and built what must have been one of the first northern commuter suburbs . . . for remember in the valley just down from this hill, towards London, were the streams, the cows and the green fields my old friend took a penny bus ride to visit every Sunday. The commuters went in by horse-bus or by train to the City.

DORIS LESSING, 'In Defence of the Underground', *London Observed*, 1992

Going home next day, he noticed as he waited on the platform for the tube to Baker Street, that the track sings as the train comes into West Hampstead, long before you can see it, and the silver lines shiver as it approaches.

BARBARA VINE, *King Solomon's Carpet*, 1991

Kilburn

The grittiness, stench and obscurity of Kilburn suddenly seemed a spiritual force – the immense force of poverty which had produced the narrow, yet intense, visions of Cockneys living in other times, with their home-made poetic philosophies – William Blake at Lambeth, Keats and Leigh Hunt at Hampstead, all the cockney characters of Dickens, dancing in the roads.

STEPHEN SPENDER, *World Within World*, 1951,
after a bad air raid in 1944

Walk a few hundred yards [from St John's Wood] and you are in Kilburn, that is to say, Ireland. Some of the pubs even have posters up for the next Irish horse-race.

WILLIAM SANSOM in *Living in London* edited by Alan Ross, 1974

Willesden Green

What a contrast did the lovely scene she [Mrs Sheppard] now gazed upon present to the squalid neighbourhood she had recently quitted!

On all sides, expanded prospects of country the most exquisite and most varied. Immediately beneath her lay Willesden, – the most charming and secluded village in the neighbourhood of the metropolis – with its scattered farm-houses, its noble granges, and its old grey church tower just peeping above a grove of rook-haunted trees.

W. HARRISON AINSWORTH, *Jack Sheppard*, 1839

Dollis Hill

Jack Sheppard and his companion left Willesden, and taking – as a blind – the direction of Harrow, returned at nightfall by a bye-lane to Neasdon, and put up at a little public-house, called the Spotted Dog. Here they remained till midnight, when, calling for their reckoning and their steeds, they left the house. It was a night well fitted to their enterprise, calm, still, and profoundly dark. As they passed beneath the thick trees that shade the road to Dollis Hill, the gloom was almost impenetrable.

W. HARRISON AINSWORTH, *Jack Sheppard*, 1839

I like travelling by Underground. This is a defiant admission. . . . This is the Jubilee line and I use it all the time. Fifteen minutes at the most to get in to the centre. The carriages are bright and new – well, almost. There are efficient indicators, Charing Cross: five minutes, three minutes, one minute. The platforms are no more littered than the streets, often less, or not at all.

DORIS LESSING, 'In Defence of the Underground',
London Observed, 1992

Neasden

Neasden! You won't be sorry that you breezed in
The traffic lights and yellow lines, the illuminated signs,
All so welcome to the borough that everybody's pleased in.
Neasden! where the birds sing in the trees-den
You can hear the blackbirds coo, so why not take the Bakerloo.
It will work out that much cheaper if you buy a seasdon.

JOHN BETJEMAN, song in 'Metro-Land'
(TV programme), 1973

Wembley Park
Change for Metropolitan line

The road to Harrow is dominated by one of London's most famous inter-war monuments, Wembley Stadium. Built in 1923 by the firm of Simpson and Ayrton, its four domed towers and scruffy concrete detailing have become the nostalgic symbol of the great days of English soccer – of a world of Brylcreem, shin pads and goalies in flat caps. The stadium was joined by the British Empire Exhibition of 1924, laid out on land to its north and intended as a permanent memorial to imperial achievement. It never attained permanence, but a number of its pavilions remain as gaunt shells along the Empire Way, sprouting occasional Egyptian doorways, classical pediments and even imperial lions. On the hillside above it, the Metroland suburb of Wembley Park looks down in disdain.

SIMON JENKINS, *The Companion Guide to Outer London*, 1981

Kingsbury

[In] Church Lane Kingsbury [there are] two churches in one church-yard, the old one very small, the new one all the prouder and in fact of more historic associations than the old building. The latter is some-times supposed to incorporate pre-Conquest work . . . the walls are more probably Norman than Saxon. Were they Saxon, they would be the only stone remains in Middlesex of so early a period. . . . The new church originally stood in Wells Street W1, and was re-erected at Kingsbury in 1933. It was a famous monument of Early Victorian Anglo-Catholicism, built in 1847. . . . Its Perp[endicular] front with NW tower and spire is big and earnest (and the spire succeeds in giving Kingsbury a genuine, not suburban look, when seen above the trees of the churchyard from across the Welsh Harp).

NIKOLAUS PEVSNER, *The Buildings of England: Middlesex*, 1951

Queensbury

When the new Metropolitan line to Stanmore was opened on 10 December 1932, one station was called Kingsbury. Two years later, a further station was opened and the name *Queensbury* was invented for it. Here then is a case of a district getting its name from a railway station!

CYRIL M. HARRIS, *What's in a Name?*, 1977

Canons Park

Near this Town, the Duke of *Chandos*, has built one of the most magnificent Palaces in *England*, with a Profusion of Expence, and so well furnish'd within, that it has hardly its Equal in *England*. The Plaistering and Gilding are done by the famous *Pargotti*, an Italian. . . . The Pillars supporting the Building are all of Marble: the great Stair-case is extremely fine, and the Steps are all of marble. . . .

The Gardens are well designed, and have a vast Variety, and the Canals are very large and noble. . . .

The Chapel is a Singularity, both in its Building and the Beauty of its Workmanship.

DANIEL DEFOE, *A Tour thro' the Whole Island of Great Britain*, 1742

At Timon's Villa let us pass the day,
Where all cry out, 'What sums are thrown away!'
So proud, so grand, of that stupendous air,
Soft and Agreeable come never there. . . .

To compass this, his building is a Town,
His pond an Ocean, his parterre a Down:
Who but must laugh, the Master when he sees,
A puny insect, shiv'ring at a breeze! . . .

The suff'ring eye inverted Nature sees,
Trees cut to Statues, Statues thick as trees,
With here a Fountain, never to be play'd,
And there a Summer-house, that knows no shade.

ALEXANDER POPE, *Moral Essay Epistle IV: To Richard Boyle, Earl of Burlington*, 1731–5 [Pope had Canons in mind when he wrote this of Timon's Villa]

Whitchurch, alias Little Stanmore, was a place of great importance in the last [eighteenth] century, during which time Canons, the palatial residence of the Duke of Chandos, rose and vanished. The church, St. Lawrence . . . now consists of a nave with a small chancel at its east end, separated by richly carved oak pillars. . . . The roof of the Chancel is painted azure, and powdered with gilt stars. . . . The rich wood carving throughout the church is by Grinling Gibbons. The nave roof is coved, divided into compartments, and frescoed by the French artists Verrio and Laguerre.*

*Handel's Chandos Anthems were written and are kept in St Lawrence's Church.

REV. JOHN HANSON SPERLING,
Church Walks in Middlesex, 1849

Stanmore

Clement Atlee lived here for 14 years until 1945 [when he moved to 10 Downing Street]. The most picturesque part of the old village [Stanmore] is round the church of St. John in Church Road. Here is an eighteenth century rectory, a barn converted into cottages, and the old Church House. . . . I was looking for a tomb surmounted by a white angel – and there it was and on its base the word 'Mackintosh', the real inscription was on a horizontal slab – this was the grave of W.S. Gilbert.

BRUCE STEVENSON, *Middlesex*, 1972

ACKNOWLEDGEMENTS

We would like to thank our families and friends who have helped us over the years during the preparation of this book, especially Sandy Marriage, Robin Ollington, Bryan Rooney, Suzanne St Albans, Anthony Sampson, Kathleen Tillotson, Malcolm Holmes of the Camden Local History Library and the staff of the North Reading Room, British Library.

The compilers and publishers gratefully acknowledge permission to reproduce the following copyright material in this book:

Julian Barnes: *Metroland*, © Julian Barnes 1980. Reprinted by permission of Jonathan Cape.

John Betjeman: 'Harrow-on-the-Hill' and 'Middlesex' (*A Few Late Chrysanthemums* 1954), from *Collected Poems*, © John Betjeman 1958. Reprinted by permission of John Murray.

Elizabeth Bowen: *The Heat of the Day*, © Elizabeth Bowen 1949. *To the North*, © Elizabeth Bowen 1932. Reprinted by permission of Jonathan Cape.

J.A. Brooks: *Ghosts of London*, © J.A. Brooks 1982. Reprinted by permission of Jarrold Publishing.

Peter Bushell: *London's Secret History*, © Peter Bushell 1983. Reprinted by permission of Constable.

Charlie Chaplin: *My Autobiography*, © Charlie Chaplin 1964. Reprinted by permission of The Bodley Head.

Alan A. Jackson: *London's Metropolitan Railway*, © Alan A. Jackson 1986. Reprinted by permission of David & Charles.

Simon Jenkins: *The Companion Guide to Outer London*, © Simon Jenkins 1981. Reprinted by permission of HarperCollins.

Doris Lessing: 'In Defence of the Underground' from *London Observed: Stories and Sketches*, © Doris Lessing 1992. Reprinted in an abridged form by permission of Jonathan Clowes on behalf of Doris Lessing, published by HarperCollins.

ACKNOWLEDGEMENTS

Christopher Logue: *London in Verse* (ed.) © Christopher Logue 1982. Reprinted by permission of Christopher Logue.

V.S. Naipaul: *The Mimic Men*, © V.S. Naipaul 1967. Reprinted by permission of Aitken, Stone & Wylie.

Hesketh Pearson: *Conan Doyle: His Life and Art*, © Hesketh Pearson 1943. Reprinted by permission of A.P. Watt on behalf of Michael Holroyd.

Nikolaus Pevsner: *The Buildings of England: Middlesex*, © Nikolaus Pevsner 1951. Reprinted by permission of Penguin Books.

William Sansom: in *Living in London* edited by Alan Ross, © William Sansom 1974. Reprinted by permission of London Magazine.

Logan Pearsall Smith: *Afterthoughts*, © Reprinted by permission of Constable.

Bruce Stevenson: *Middlesex*, © Bruce Stevenson 1972. Reprinted by permission of B.T. Batsford.

Barbara Vine: *King Solomon's Carpet*, © Kingsmarkham Enterprises Ltd 1991. Reprinted by permission of Penguin Books.

Jill Paton Walsh: *The Fireweed*, © Jill Paton Walsh 1969. Reprinted by permission of Thomas Nelson.

Ben Weinreb and Christopher Hibbert: *The London Encyclopaedia*, © Ben Weinreb and Christopher Hibbert 1983. Reprinted by permission of Macmillan London.

H.G. Wells: *Love and Mr Lewisham*, © H.G. Wells 1900. Reprinted by permission of A.P. Watt on behalf of The Literary Executors of the Estate of H.G. Wells.

The publishers have made every effort to contact copyright holders where they can be found. The publishers will be happy to include any missing copyright acknowledgements in future editions.